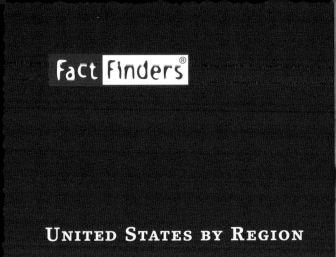

Fact Finders®

UNITED STATES BY REGION

People and Places of the

WEST

by Danielle Smith-Llera

Consultant:
Dr. David Lanegran
John S. Holl Professor of Geography
Macalester College
St. Paul, Minnesota

CAPSTONE PRESS
a capstone imprint

Fact Finders Books are published by Capstone Press,
1710 Roe Crest Drive, North Mankato, Minnesota 56003
www.mycapstone.com

Library of Congress Cataloging-in-Publication Data
Library of Congress Cataloging-in-Publication Data
Names: Smith-Llera, Danielle, 1971- author.
Title: People and places of the West / by Danielle Smith-Llera.
Description: North Mankato, Minnesota : Capstone Press, 2017. | Series: Fact
    finders. United States by region | Includes bibliographical references and
    index. | Audience: Grades 4 to 6.? | Audience: Ages 9 to 12.?
Identifiers: LCCN 2016010776| ISBN 9781515724414 (library binding) | ISBN
    9781515724469 (pbk.) | ISBN 9781515724513 (ebook pdf))
Subjects: LCSH: West (U.S.)—Juvenile literature.
Classification: LCC F596 .S66 2017 | DDC 978—dc23
LC record available at http://lccn.loc.gov/2016010776

Editorial Credits
Angie Kaelberer, editor; Cynthia Della-Rovere, designer; Svetlana Zhurkin, media researcher;
Laura Manthe, production specialist

Photo Credits
Corbis: David Stoecklein, cover (top); Courtesy Scotts Bluff National Monument, 13; Granger, NYC, 10–11; iStockphoto: Cynthia Baldauf, 22; Newscom: WENN/ZOB/CB2, 29; North Wind Picture Archives, 8–9; Shutterstock: Arina P. Habich, 25, Can Balcioglu, 21, Deymos.HR, 26–27, Everett Historical, 12, 19, Jim in SC, 18, Lee Prince, 15, Luciano Mortula, 23, Rigucci, cover (bottom), Stacey Lynn Payne, 6, topseller, 17

Design and Map Elements by Shutterstock

Printed in the United States of America.
009672F16.

Table of Contents

Introduction 4

Chapter 1: History and Growth 8

Chapter 2: Land and Climate 14

Chapter 3: Jobs and Economy 20

Chapter 4: People and Culture 24

Glossary 30

Read More 31

Internet Sites 31

Index 32

INTRODUCTION

People in the West might see a cactus, mountains, forests, or even a volcano or a **glacier**. Snow may cover their cities, or they might wear short sleeves all year. They might even need to wear rain boots and sunscreen on the same day.

This huge region includes 11 states. They are Alaska, Hawaii, Washington, Oregon, Idaho, Wyoming, Montana, Colorado, California, Utah, and Nevada.

Populations of the western states vary. The West includes both of the states with the most and fewest numbers of people. The state with the most people is California and the one with the fewest is Wyoming. The others fall somewhere in between.

glacier: a large, slow-moving sheet of ice

Washington

Montana

Oregon

Idaho

Wyoming

Nevada

Utah

Colorado

California

Pacific
Ocean

Alaska

Hawaii

Alaska is shown much
smaller than its actual size.

The West Region by Rank

Let's see how the states in the West compare to each other. This chart includes each state and ranks it by population and area. Each state's capital and nickname are also listed. Some nicknames make sense. California is called the Golden State because many gold mines were located there. But why is Utah the Beehive State? You may have to do some research to find out the reason!

Washington state is nicknamed the Evergreen State. The area is covered with evergreen forests.

State	Population	Rank	Square Miles	Rank	Capital	Nickname
Alaska	736,732	48	656,424	1	Juneau	Last Frontier
California	38,802,500	1	163,707	3	Sacramento	Golden State
Colorado	5,355,866	22	104,100	8	Denver	Centennial State
Hawaii	1,419,561	40	6,459	47	Honolulu	Aloha State
Idaho	1,634,464	39	83,574	14	Boise	Gem State
Montana	1,023,579	44	147,046	4	Helena	Treasure State
Nevada	2,839,099	35	110,567	7	Carson City	Silver State
Oregon	3,970,239	27	98,386	9	Salem	Beaver State
Utah	2,942,902	33	84,904	13	Salt Lake City	Beehive State
Washington	7,061,530	13	71,303	18	Olympia	Evergreen State
Wyoming	584,153	51	97,818	10	Cheyenne	Equality State

Chapter 1

HISTORY AND GROWTH

For thousands of years, the land gave western American Indian tribes all they needed to live. The Chumash settled along the Pacific coast. Paiutes, Shoshones, and Utes lived in the desert. The Nez Perce lived near rivers in present-day Washington and Idaho. Further north were the Tlingits of Alaska.

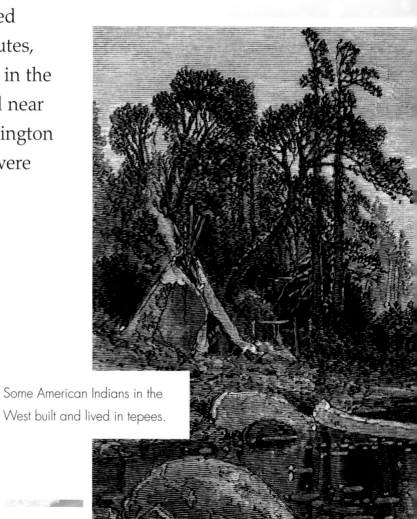

Some American Indians in the West built and lived in tepees.

Near the coast women collected nuts and berries from the forests. Men fished in the rivers and the Pacific Ocean. On the open **plains**, men hunted deer and buffalo with bows and arrows. Women cooked and preserved meat and turned hides into clothing. Some tribes lived in wooden tepee frames covered with grasses or animal skins.

plains: a large, flat area of land with few trees

Europeans Arrive

In 1542 Spanish explorer Juan Rodríguez Cabrillo and his crew were the first Europeans to visit the Pacific Coast. In 1769 Spanish settlers built a military fort in what is now San Diego. The fort was the first permanent European settlement on the Pacific Coast. The Spanish also built **missions** to spread the Christian religion to the American Indians.

mission: a church or settlement where religious leaders live and work

Other explorers were interested in the West. In the 1700s Russian explorers sailed along the Pacific coast into Alaska. They traded with American Indians for sea otter furs. English and French traders set up trading posts on the Columbia River. They collected furs to trade for tea and silk from China.

Spanish explorers chose San Diego Bay for building a military fort.

Western Expansion

The U.S. government wanted to claim western lands. In 1803 President Thomas Jefferson made the Louisiana Purchase. He bought a huge piece of land from the French. It included large parts of Wyoming, Montana, and Colorado.

The United States took over more of the West in 1846. That year Great Britain and the United States signed the Oregon Treaty. The agreement set a border between the western United States and British Canada. Two years later the United States won the Mexican-American War. The United States received land that became the states of California, Nevada, and Utah, as well as parts of Colorado and Wyoming.

During the Gold Rush, some miners used a device called a sluice to collect gold.

Thousands of Americans dreamed of better lives in the West Settlers in covered wagons made the difficult journey west on the Oregon Trail. In 1848 gold was discovered in the Sierra Nevada Mountains. Thousands of people moved west hoping to strike it rich during the Gold Rush.

The United States also spread beyond Canada and the Pacific Ocean. It bought Alaska from Russia in 1867 and added the territory of Hawaii in 1900. In 1959 Hawaii and Alaska became the last states admitted to the Union.

The Oregon Trail

The Oregon Trail began in Missouri and stretched about 2,200 miles (3,500 kilometers) to Oregon. As many as 500,000 settlers traveled it between the early 1840s and 1870. American Indian routes formed much of the trail. The trail included the South Pass, which was an easier path through the Rocky Mountains.

People traveled in covered wagons pulled by oxen. They formed wagon trains of up to 1,000 people for safety and support. The journey took between four to six months. At least 20,000 settlers died during the trip, most from diseases.

By 1870 railroad travel replaced the covered wagons. Today, parts of the trail can still be seen in areas of the West.

Chapter 2

LAND AND CLIMATE

The West includes forests, deserts, and mountain ranges. The Rocky Mountains spread from Canada to New Mexico. East of the mountains are the Great Plains. They include much of Montana, Wyoming, and Colorado.

The Great Basin is a desert region that makes up most of Nevada and a large part of Utah. It also includes parts of California, Oregon, Idaho, and Wyoming. Death Valley, California, is in the Great Basin. It's the hottest and driest place in the United States. Its temperatures can reach more than 120 degrees Fahrenheit (49 degrees Celsius)! And it gets only 2 inches (5 centimeters) of rain each year.

FACT

The world's hottest temperature was recorded at Death Valley on July 10, 1913. It was 134 degrees F (57 degrees C).

Other parts of the West get lots of moisture. Hoh Rain Forest in Washington receives at least 150 inches (381 cm) of rain and snow each year. But that's nothing compared to some areas in Alaska and Hawaii. One area in Alaska averages 237 inches (602 cm) of rain and snow. Hawaii is even rainier. Its wettest place is Mount Waialeale on Kauai island. About 450 inches (1,143 cm) of rain falls on the mountain's peak every year!

Mount Waialeale in Hawaii has beautiful waterfalls that fall from the mountain. This is one of the wettest areas in the world.

Mountains, Lakes, and Rivers

North America's highest mountain range can be found in Alaska. It is called the Alaska Range. At 20,310 feet (6,190 meters), Denali is the tallest. Many large glaciers are located in the mountains.

The Sierra Nevada mountains are the home of Lake Tahoe. It's North America's largest mountain lake. In summer people swim and paddleboard in the lake. In winter they slide down mountainsides on tubes, skis, and snowboards.

Major rivers cross the West too. The Columbia flows from Canada to the Pacific Ocean in Oregon. The Colorado River begins in the Rocky Mountains of Colorado and flows southwest into Mexico.

FACT

No roads can cross the rugged land surrounding Alaska's Glacier Bay National Park near Juneau. The only way to see the glaciers is by boat or airplane.